Fat ...
Babies

LAUGHING ELEPHANT

MMXIX

"Hello, little gopher," say the baby goats.

The prize colt takes candy from Rusty's basket.

The ducklings play "Follow the Leader" in the pond.

Um-m-m! That fresh milk will taste good!

What a lot of vegetables the bunnies found!

Who left the gate open? Now the pigs will eat the cake.

The kittens have fun with the farmer's hat.

"Oh, look at the worm we found!" say the chicks.

The squirrel will put this acorn away for winter.

"What nice ripe grapes!" says the rooster.

All the goslings want to swim in the tiny pond.

The baby donkey makes friends with the farm pets.

The playful calf broke loose and upset the pail.

"Flowers smell good enough to eat," say the lambs.

ISBN/EAN: 9781595838865

THIS PRODUCT CONFORMS TO CPSIA 2008
FIRST PRINTING · SECOND EDITION · PRINTED IN CHINA · ALL RIGHTS RESERVED
THIS IS A REPRINT OF A BOOK FIRST PUBLISHED IN 1940.

LAUGHING ELEPHANT
3645 INTERLAKE AVENUE NORTH SEATTLE, WA 98103

LAUGHINGELEPHANT.COM